T0419194

Copyright @ 2023 Neuro Navigation
All rights reserved. No Part of this publication may be reproduced, distributed, or transmitted in any form or by any means, including photocopying, recording, or other electronic or mechanical methods, without the prior written permission of the publisher, except in the case of brief quotations embodied in critical reviews and certain other noncommercial uses permitted by copyright law. For permission requests, email or write to the publisher, info@neuro-naviation.com or send a written request to:

Neuro Navigation Publishing
777 N. Jefferson Street
Milwaukee, WI 53202

Introduction

This is the first book in a series about Kelly's experiences. Kelly is a neurodivergent learner in a neurotypical school. She shows the challenges and triumphs of her journey to succeed at school and make friends. She also learns about her specific learning disabilities. This book uses dyslexia friendly font.

Specific Learning Disabilities

Receiving   Processing

Communicating

Recalling

Reading   Auditory processing

Writing   Sensory / motor

Spelling   Emotional

Math   Social

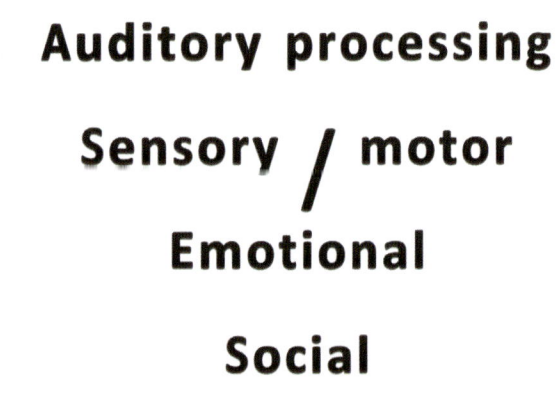

Specific learning disabilities:

Dyslexia:
Difficult to read, write, and
spell words.

Dysgraphia:
Struggle to write legibly
and coherently.

Dyspraxia:
Difficult to coordinate muscles,
and balancing.

Dyscalculia:
Challenge to understand and solve
math problems.

Kelly is **clever.**

Kelly is always kind and fair to friends.
All were amazed how fast Kelly figured out puzzles.

Kelly didn't feel she was **clever.**

Because she could not read or write like her friends.

At school, kids often laughed when Kelly read out loud.
This made her feel sad and not **clever**.

But you *are* **clever**, Kelly!

She figured out how to not get called on by her teacher.

Kelly was afraid kids at school would find out she could not read.

Kelly tried to keep the secret that she could not read.

She pretended her belly hurt to avoid school and playing with her friends.

Soon Kelly became very lonely.

Kelly's mom took her to a doctor.
The doctor wanted to find out why Kelly could not read.

The doctor said that Kelly is **clever!**

Kelly has *dyslexia.*
This means she needs accommodations to
help her learn at school.

Fun questions about Clever Girl!

1. What cool toys does Kelly have in her room?

2. What did Kelly do that amazed her friends?

3. Why did Kelly feel she was not clever?

4. Why did Kelly not want her friends to know she could not read or write?

5. What did Kelly do so her teacher would not call on her in class?

Fun questions about Clever Girl!

6. What does dyslexia mean?

7. What kind of bear is in Kelly's toy box?

8. What fun things did Kelly like to do?

9. What helped Kelly learn to read?

If you're having *trouble in school* tell someone and *get help!*
www.Neuro-Navigation.com

More books are available at www.Neuro-Navigation.com

Why should you read Kelly's book: "The Child Who Learned Differently"

The Child Who Learned Differently:

Parents and caregivers of neurodivergent learners will gain a better understanding of the challenges faced by neurodivergent children and discover strategies to support them.

Educators and school administrators will read the book to gain insights to create an inclusive learning environment for neurodivergent learners.

Neurodivergent learners will relate to this book, feel less alone, find inspiration, discover strategies, and courage for self-advocacy to succeed.

Organization leaders who have neurodivergent learners on their workforce will have insight for reviewing their procedures to find a inclusive work environment for all.